Charged with Grandeur

Sermons and Practices for Delighting in God's Creation

Christopher Keating

CSS Publishing Company, Inc.
Lima, Ohio

CHARGED WITH GRANDEUR

FIRST EDITION
Copyright © 2016
by CSS Publishing Co., Inc.

Published by CSS Publishing Company, Inc., Lima, Ohio 45807. All rights reserved. No part of this publication may be reproduced in any manner whatsoever without the prior permission of the publisher, except in the case of brief quotations embodied in critical articles and reviews. Inquiries should be addressed to: CSS Publishing Company, Inc., Permissions Department, 5450 N. Dixie Highway, Lima, Ohio 45807.

Scripture quotations marked (NRSV) are from the New Revised Standard Version of the Bible. Copyright 1989 by the Division of Christian Education of the National Council of the Churches of Christ in the USA, Nashville, Thomas Nelson Publishers © 1989. Used by permission. All rights reserved.

Library of Congress Cataloging-in-Publication Data

Names: Keating, Christopher W., author.
Title: Charged with grandeur : sermons and practices for delighting in God's creation / Christopher W. Keating.
Description: FIRST EDITION. | Lima : CSS Publishing Company, 2016.
Identifiers: LCCN 2016013895 | ISBN 9780788028335 (pbk. : alk. paper)
Subjects: LCSH: Creation--Sermons. | Ecotheology--Sermons.
Classification: LCC BS651 .K35 2016 | DDC 231.7/65--dc23
LC record available at https://lccn.loc.gov/2016013895

For more information about CSS Publishing Company resources, visit our website at www.csspub.com, email us at csr@csspub.com, or call (800) 241-4056.

e-book:
ISBN-13: 978-0-7880-2873-1
ISBN-10: 0-7880-2873-1

ISBN-13: 978-0-7880-2833-5
ISBN-10: 0-7880-2833-2

PRINTED IN US

*To my mother, Lois Keating and
my late father, Frank C. Keating.
You taught me to celebrate creation as we sang
"Of rocks and trees, of skies and seas,
God's hand the wonders wrought."*

Table of Contents

Introduction	7
Chapter One The Calling of Ecological Disciples: Visiting Our Stuff	9
Chapter Two Casting Out into the Deep	15
Chapter Three Listening to the Song of Creation	21
Chapter Four Paths of Danger	29
Chapter Five Bread from Heaven	35
Chapter Six Charged with Granduer	41
Chapter Seven What Sort of Animal Are We, Anyway? A Communion Meditation	47
Chapter Eight Uncovering Our Ears	51
Chapter Nine A Festival of Hymns Celebrating Creation	59
Major Sources	65

Introduction

THE WORLD is charged with the grandeur of God.
It will flame out, like shining from shook foil;
It gathers to a greatness, like the ooze of oil crushed.
— "God's Grandeur" by Gerard Manley Hopkins

The outlook is gloomy. News of greenhouse warming, ocean acidification, air pollution, spoiled water, and urban food deserts grabs our attention daily. These are reminders of the varied environmental crises facing the Earth. It is easy to be pessimistic.

Yet God calls us to be a people of hope. We are a people entrusted with proclaiming good news by a God who takes delight in creation. If we are to take seriously the care of creation, we must rekindle our delight in the creation God calls good. The church needs to celebrate the goodness of creation while also discovering new ways of caring for our Earth home.

Within these pages, I set out to help the church recover its appreciation of the grandeur of God. These sermons include resources designed to provide a starting place for vital theological conversations about the environment. They model one way of helping Christians hear God's call to stewardship. I've been helped by the writers of the "Season of Creation" liturgical resources.[1] These writers are challenging the church to connect its worship with the environmental crisis. As they note, "We are challenged to return to our biblical roots to rediscover our intimate connections with creation. We return to see ourselves again as part of the very Earth from which we are made."[2]

My gratitude to Dr. Anna Case-Winters and Dr. Theodore Hiebert for helping develop this project as part of McCormick Theological Seminary's Certificate In Environmental Ministry and Leadership. I'm grateful for the encouragement provided by Dr. J. Clinton McCann at Eden Theological Seminary for careful reading; to my wife, the Rev. Carol McCracken Keating and our children for their persistent encouragement; and my friends and colleagues the Rev. Dr. J. Patrick Vaughn and Dr. Gary Neal Hanson for their reflections.

The first sermon was originally written for the Church of the Brethren magazine, *Messenger*. The next four sermons were part of a "Celebrating Creation" sermon series in September and October 2013 at Woodlawn Chapel Presbyterian Church in Wildwood, Missouri — a congregation that honors the impulse for celebrating creation and caring for the Earth in its worship and life. Other sermons reflect my continuing interest in linking preaching with environmental concerns. Included are suggestions for reflections and a weekly "Take Action" practice that moves the congregation into a specific ecological practice.

---

1. www.seasonofcreation.com
2. See "Celebrating Christ with Creation — A Theology of Worship for the Season of Creation" http://seasonofcreation.com/theology/accessed November 27, 2014.

Chapter One

The Calling of Ecological Disciples: Visiting Our Stuff

(A version of this introduction first appeared as an article in the May 2013 edition of *Messenger* magazine, the official publication of the Church of the Brethren and is reprinted with permission.)

> *He called the crowd with his disciples and said to them, If any want to become my followers, let them deny themselves and take up their cross and follow me. For those who want to save their life will lose, and those who lose their life for my sake, and for the sake of the gospel, will save it. For what will it profit them to gain the whole world and forfeit their life?*
> — Mark 8:34-35

Just six hours into my trip to Chicago, and I was headed to the dump.

Many of my friends in St. Louis were packing their bags for sunnier, and less smelly, destinations. Spring break is supposed to take people to beaches or ski slopes — not landfills and waste sites.

But here I was — not on vacation, but taking a class — discovering the impact humans have had on this corner of the planet, and discovering new ways of helping churches develop environmental ministries. Organized by McCormick Theological Seminary in Chicago, I was enrolled in a class on environmental ministry and leadership. It's a broad topic, but for starters we took a tour of a few toxic waste sites in Chicago.

In a way, the tour took me back to my stuff, while also calling me again to the work of discipleship.

A volunteer from a neighborhood environmental group guided us past giant industrial plants, slag piles, and abandoned steel

9

mills on the city's southeast side. We boarded a yellow school bus to drive around economically depressed neighborhoods and trash-filled vacant lots. Our guide showed us evidence of polluted waters; inviting us to see huge mounds of landfills no longer used for dumping. He showed us acres of buried toxins covered by dirt and surrounded by menacing chain link and razor wire fences. With the city's magnificent skyline soaring in the background, we saw miles of former wetland spaces that were now wastelands.

Since my family had lived in Chicago until the early 1960s, I felt like visiting these dumping sites was akin to visiting my family's ancestral ruins. The area, used for the dumping or incinerating of trash since the early 1900s, is surrounded by vacated manufacturing plants. Immense waste areas remain as remnants of the area's past. I looked at the mounds and knew our family's garbage was still in there, slowly decaying. The footprint of existence had extended to these landfills, spaces that are now being turned into golf courses.

I'll be honest. Visiting the dump was not my idea of how to spend a day in Chicago. Going to museums, exploring neighborhoods, touching base with relatives — just about anything else would have been preferable to looking at garbage. But the visit to "my" old stuff stirred my imagination. It stayed with me. Going to the landfill was a visual reminder of why we are called to care for the environment. In a visceral way, it underscored for me what it means to hear Jesus say, "If any want to become my followers, let them deny themselves and take up their cross and follow me... for what will it profit them to gain the whole world and forfeit their life?" (Mark 8:34, 36).

That visit made me think about carrying a cross, while caring for the environment.

On average, Americans produce over four pounds of trash each day. (If I get around to cleaning my basement, I'll blow the national average immediately, but that is another story.) Our stuff has to go someplace. While the answers to our ecological dilemmas are not clear, we can begin by discerning God's call to a cross-shaped life. While Jesus didn't appoint a congregational "Green Team," giving them authority over recycling and conserving, he did call disciples to follow him. He speaks of the high cost of discipleship, and how it involves a change of priorities. In chapter 8 of Mark's gospel, he begins to openly discuss the meaning of costly discipleship.

After feeding the 4,000 and curing the blind man at Bethsaida, Jesus provides specific instructions to the disciples, opening their eyes and feeding their souls. He asks the disciples, "Who do you say that I am?" They answer, "The Messiah," which immediately results in Jesus sternly instructing them not to tell anyone about him.

What happens next is particularly intriguing, however. While he has told them to be quiet, Jesus quite openly explores the fine print of what being Messiah is truly about. He tells them that being Messiah isn't about political grandeur and claiming power. It is about suffering, being rejected, even being killed. The job description of the Messiah, according to Jesus, is quite plain — just as it is for those who wish to follow him. Jesus is clear: "If any want to become my followers, let them deny themselves and take up their cross and follow me."

It's the implications of that verse which aren't always so clear. Normally, when someone says "I've got my cross to bear," they are referring to an illness, to a particularly obnoxious relative, or talking about a car with a funky clutch. Instead, as scholars point out, this is about placing God's priorities ahead of ours. It is about seeking first the kingdom. It includes caring for others and deepening our care for creation.

When I looked at the grassy slopes of buried garbage, I became aware that perhaps denying ourselves may lead to engaging our consumer world that keeps urging us to buy more and more stuff. But it is possible that we could gain a world of stuff yet lose our planet in the process.

While the Old Testament — particularly in Genesis and the wisdom literature — abounds with images of creation and nature, ecological inferences in the New Testament are not always immediately clear. A resource such as *The Green Bible*,[1] which lists environmental references in green ink, can be helpful in locating scriptural guidance for earth care. But perhaps the best way to explore our calling to care for each other and creation is to hear again Jesus' invitation to radical discipleship and more simple lifestyles.

For twenty-first-century Christians, denying ourselves should include increasing our awareness of how we care for the earth. That is our calling. Reducing, reusing, recycling are not just words our kids learn in school, but words that should also be echoed in the church's worship and life. Picking up our cross includes conversations about earth care at home and Sunday school, in legislatures and church picnics.

In Mark 8, Jesus opened the ears of the deaf and cleared the eyes of the blind. Now he broadens the vision of the disciples to see the true nature of his work. He calls them to pick up their crosses and to follow him in pathways of service and self-giving love. The cross is a potent sign of death, as visceral a symbol of decay as those landfills I visited. As Dietrich Bonhoeffer is famously quoted, "When Christ calls a man (or woman), he bids him (her) to come and die." But the cross also leads to new life, resurrection power, and deeper communion with Christ. Being a disciple requires giving of ourselves, taking up the symbolic emblem of death as our own personal crest in order that we might find true life.

This is the sum of the Christian life. It is an action of setting down and picking up. In the words of Dawn Ottoni Wilhelm, "The challenge and blessing of Jesus' all-encompassing call insists on a radical reorientation of our lives that draws us into a closer relationship with him."[2]

Picking up our cross may lead us to the landfill, but it also leads to new life.

---

1. *The Green Bible, New Revised Standard Version* (San Francisco: HarperCollins, 2008), see also www.greenletterbible.com
2. Dawn Ottani Wilhelm, *Preaching the Gospel of Mark: Proclaiming the Power of God* (Louisville: Westminster/John Knox Press, 2008), p. 157.

Questions for Reflection
1. Do you know where your trash goes? Working with a group from your church, research the path your trash takes on its way to the dump. Where are the landfills in your area?

2. How does your congregation show care for God's creation? What obstacles are present that hinder deepening your congregation's commitment to Earth stewardship?

3. What steps are involved in creating Earth care conversations within your congregation?

Take Action

1. Gather a small group to begin your congregation's environmental ministry. Adult groups might begin by watching the documentary "Trashed — No Place for Waste," which is available on DVD for purchase. Narrated by Jeremy Irons, the movie depicts the mountains of waste that threaten the Earth's environment.

2. Using resources from your denomination, consider the steps involved in becoming a more environmentally friendly or "green" congregation. Visit your denominational webpage or www.webofcreation.org for ideas on how to initiate an Earth care ministry within your congregation.

3. Consider hosting a "bring your own coffee mug" Sunday rather than using foam or paper cups. Look for ways of reducing the amount of plastic your church uses on a regular basis.

Chapter Two

Casting Out into the Deep

Luke 5:1-11; Job 38:1-18

Ocean Sunday

Today's worship space includes signs of the sea. Fragments of shells where creatures lived, fragile starfish reminding us of the imperiled oceans, nets which call to mind the fishermen's vocation are all placed against a blue cloth that calls to mind the vast depths of the ocean. As the sermon continues, a video of undersea life can be played to encourage reflection on God's gift of the abundant ocean. Jesus calls the disciples to go back into the deep and demonstrates the abundance of God's creation. He reminds them that our calling is to act as disciples who delight in creation and who respond to God's grace through acts of risky faith.

Earlier this year, I picked up a copy of *The Green Bible*.[1] Many of us grew up with Bibles we called the "red letter Bible," those versions of the King James Version or the RSV with the words of Jesus in red. *The Green Bible* is a similar idea. Its editors have combed the scriptures and highlighted verses dealing with creation in green. It includes over 1,000 references to the Earth and caring for creation.

Read scripture carefully and you find that caring for creation is at the very core of our faith. For many reasons, however, we don't talk much about caring for creation in church. My hunch is that many of us do care a great deal about the Earth. But often we are overwhelmed by the sheer magnitude of the problem. Where do we start? How can we make a difference?

Belden Lane is a Presbyterian minister who teaches at Saint Louis University. He has said that perhaps the best way is to begin learning how to delight in creation. It's part of our heritage as Presbyterians. John Calvin, rarely called an environmentalist, wrote that "if now I seek to despoil the land of what God has given it to sustain human beings, then I am seeking as much as I can to do away with God's goodness."[2] As Lane has written, "We will not be able to save, after all, what we have not learned to love."[3] By delighting in creation, we may hear God's call to us in new ways.

We may also learn where we have gone wrong so that we can begin again. Delighting in creation allows us to consider, with Job, our relationship to creation. It allows us to break forth in song — delighting, praising, and loving God.

So let's begin by going deep. Dive into the sea and celebrate the beauty of God's gifts. The oceans make up 70% of the Earth's surface. The ocean is the earth's largest habitat — 99% of our planet's living space. According to the National Oceanic and Atmospheric Administration, more than 50% of all species live in the ocean. We tend to forget just how vital the ocean is to the carbon cycle. It absorbs 22 million tons of CO_2 each day…and provides 50% of the oxygen the Earth requires. The seas are important — and increasing acidification of the world's oceans should concern each of us. The oceans are vast, beautiful, and mysterious, yet also fragile, and in some places endangered by human folly.

(As the sermon progressed, underwater images were displayed on a video screen.)

In scripture, the sea is a place where God's power pushes back the forces of chaos and where God is at work. It is a place of danger — filled with untamed beasts and deadly storms. But the sea is also where God's people began again in their Exodus from Egypt, a place of creation and re-creation. No one should be surprised that Jesus' ministry is filled with images of water, and that it is at the lakeshore that he began his ministry.

We tend to push the lake into the background in this story. While technically not an ocean, of course, the Sea of Galilee was viewed with oceans as being part of God's vast storehouse of water.[4] The sea is a place where we are called to "go deep," and discern what God is calling us to do.

One summer in seminary I worked as an intern at a church in California just blocks from the ocean. One of my jobs was to lead a youth group Bible study on the beach once a week. Life as a seminary intern can be tough! Each week we would load up kids in a bright orange VW minivan and drive a few blocks to the beach, where my partner and I would do our best to keep the kids interested in Bible study. At first, we didn't have much luck.

The thought was — if Jesus called disciples by the shore of the sea, why couldn't we? But as my friend and I told our supervising pastors, Jesus didn't have to compete with girls in two-piece bathing suits. It was actually pretty frustrating. We'd gather the kids in a circle around the beach and have their attention for two seconds. But it all changed when we ditched the prescribed study and began asking real questions — questions that "went deep." We left the safety of the shore behind. In the beauty of that place, we worked on developing authentic Christian community. With the disciples, we asked, "Where is God calling me to follow?"

That question guides the church over and over again. It is what guides our desires to reach out in mission and ministry: How can we go deep with our community? And, as we view these incredible images of God's sea creatures, it should prompt us to celebrate creation by understanding our contribution to the ocean's environmental crisis.

Let me ask you that question today: Where is God calling you to follow?

Jesus looks at the results of Simon's disappointing night's work. The fishermen have nothing but empty nets. Luke doesn't tell us what they're saying under their breath, but I think we can imagine the sort of words sleepless hard working fishermen might use to convey their frustration. They are disappointed, tired, and more than a bit worried about how these empty nets would pay the bills.

Yet the promise of God was not far from them.

On the lakeshore, God comes to them, calling them to go back to the place of their disappointment so that they might be amazed. The sea is not just a place of creation, but also re-creation... a place where God is beginning the work creating a new community.

Jesus, who turned their boats into a makeshift pulpit, now provides a whopper of a sermon conclusion. He looks at their empty nets and commands them to go back out into the sea. That's right: go right back to the place of your disappointment. Peter isn't impressed, but for some reason he does what Jesus asks him to do.

Go out into the deep. Take a risk. Seek out the miracle of God's creation. Be astonished and delighted in what you find.

Well, you can't argue with the results. As soon as the nets are placed into the water, the fish swarm. The guys struggle to pull the nets into the boats, straining against the weight of the fish. The boats begin to sink, the fish push against the nets. It was, quite literally, a tipping point for those fishermen... they're overwhelmed by the sight of God's abundance.

That is part of the good news in this story: The sea is filled with reminders of God's abundance. The nets hauled in all sorts of fish and sea creatures — a sign of God is at work, despite our disappointments! The response is amazing. Never did these fishermen see so many fish! Their families, their friends, their neighbors, all the people they are called to feed will have enough to eat. God's abundance provides for all. That is a sure sign of what God is doing, and it is word of comfort to the church.

But the story does not end there. The story gets a bit more interesting as Peter gets weak in the knees — the sight of the fish is just too overwhelming. He confesses, "I'm a sinner."

In the stunning face of creation's beauty, Peter is astonished and made aware of his humanity. It is an arresting image. How often have we looked into the deep beauty of God's creation and thought, "This is amazing... yet how have we sinned by damaging your creation, Lord? We have polluted your good seas. We have been greedy in taking more than we needed. Lord, we have not always thought of how you would have us care for creation." Our inattention to the seas has damaged God's creation.

But notice that Jesus didn't judge Peter — instead, he told him not to be afraid and to follow. He holds the sea and its gifts as a reminder of the web of God's creation — a symbol of the way the kingdom of God is breaking into the world. Jesus stood on the lakeshore and called Peter, James, and John to join him in the work of new creation — to share food with the hungry, to care for the wounded, to reach out to those who had been abandoned, to seek first the kingdom of God.

Let me ask again, "Where is God calling you to follow? Where is God calling you to make a change in your corner of the world?" Where are we called to "go deep" and respond to the cry of the ocean's distress?

As we celebrate the depths of creation, let us listen for the voice of one who is calling us to go deep into those waters — plunging ahead, casting our nets, continuing the work of creation.

---

1. *The Green Bible, New Revised Standard Version* (San Francisco: HarperCollins, 2008), see also www.greenletterbible.com
2. Quoted in Belden C. Lane, *Ravished by Beauty* (New York: Oxford University Press, 2011), p. 29.
3. *Ibid.*, p. 225.
4. See Theodore Hiebert, *The Living Ocean: Season of Creation Week 1*, www.workingpreacher.org.

Questions for Reflection
1. Luke alone has Jesus teaching from the lakeshore. One scholar suggests that Luke may be making a theological point — that the lakeshore is a manifestation of Jesus' power.* In any case, it provides a visual reminder of the vastness of creation. Thinking back on moments when you have walked along a beach, what has struck you about the power of God in relationship to the ocean or other large body of water?
2. The disciples' empty nets symbolized their disappointment. In following Jesus by "diving deep" and caring for creation, what signs of disappointment could we encounter?
3. Ocean acidification is one critical challenge to the abundance of God's underwater creation. How much do you know about it?

Take Action
1. Do an internet search for groups in your area that focus on restoring clean streams and creeks. Often such groups schedule work days to clear trash from streams and rivers.

2. Instead of letting down our nets, perhaps Jesus is calling to take up our canoes and trash bags and volunteer in a significant way. Identify yourselves as part of your church's "stream team."

*Joseph A. Fitzmeyer, *The Gospel According to Luke*, Vol. 1 (Doubleday and Company, 1981), p. 565.

Chapter Three

Listening to the Song of Creation

Genesis 2:4b-15; Psalm 104 (selections)

In creation, God calls humans into deep relationship with the creation as tillers of the garden God has given us so that we may share God's delight in creation and discover the depth of God's love for all. Today in the worship space, there are signs of the flora and fauna of creation. Cloth representing rivers is placed on a table near the front, along with rocks, small trees (or branches), and various woodland creatures that comprise the good garden of creation.

I'm going to go down on record today as the preacher who told his congregation to take a hike!

Last week, we dove deep into the ocean to celebrate the beauty of the oceans. We marveled at the beauty of the seas. We listened for Jesus calling us to go deep into the sea — and learned what it means for us to give thanks to God for oceans, seas, and great bodies of water. Today we move to dry land, to terra firma. We open our ears to listen for God's voice in creation.

So let's take a hike!

There's something profoundly spiritually rewarding in meandering — in walking without a purpose except to notice where God is at work in creation. Meandering brings us close to the work God does — it is why John Calvin, even stodgy old Calvin himself, said that the world is the theater of God's glory. Calvin remarked: "There is not one blade of grass, there is no color in this world that is not intended to make us rejoice."

One of the joys that I have experienced in this church family has been our annual family retreat to Mound Ridge, the Camp and Conference Center of the Presbytery of Giddings-Lovejoy near

St. James, Missouri. At our first retreat, I worked hard to schedule every minute. The group was kind and gracious in their participation but by the end of the weekend, they told me what they most wanted to do was nothing. They wanted to meander, to wander... sort of a Presbyterian version of *Eat, Pray, Love*.

Meander down a path and watch the sun set over the water or listen to the water lapping at the edge of a lake. Discover the squirrels running up a tree and notice the fog hanging close to a low spot. Go out and take a hike, listening for chuffing of animals and sing with the psalmist:

> *O Lord my God, you are very great! You cause the grass to grow for the cattle, and plants for the people to use, to bring forth food from the earth!*
> (Psalm 104:1b, 14)

Take a walk and behold the work of our God.

Writer and preacher Barbara Brown Taylor once remarked that what drew her deep into faith were not so much the "believing" parts of Christianity, but the "beholding parts." In her memoir, *Leaving Church*, Taylor says:

> *The parts of the Christian story that had drawn me into the church were not the believing parts but the beholding parts. "Behold, I bring you good news of great joy..." "Behold the Lamb of God..." "Behold, I stand at the door and knock..." Whether the narratives starred hayseed shepherds confronted by hosts of glittering angels or desert pilgrims watching something like a dove descend upon a man in a river as a voice from heaven called things that were clearly beyond belief... While I understood both why and how the early church decided to wrap those mysteries in protective layers of orthodox belief, the beliefs never seized my heart the way mysteries did.*[1]

Take a hike; behold the good works of God! Let the mysteries seize your heart. Behold the joy of Jesus' love as the trees change. Behold the depth of Christ's mercy even as the mosquitoes bite and the chiggers dig into your ankles. Behold the mystery of faith as you meander through creation.

And as you take a hike, pay close attention. You may discover what has been missing from your life for a very long time. Pay attention and discover God's voice calling out to you — perhaps for the first time, or for the first time in a long time. Take a hike into the world and listen for the song of creation as it beats out the notes of God's grace.

Perhaps you may never have noticed that there are two stories of creation in Genesis. Actually, the Bible has several accounts of creation, including Psalm 104. Most of us know the story from Genesis 1, that poem of creation… "In the beginning when God created the heavens and the earth, the earth was a formless void…" The actions of God dominate this account. Creation is orderly and specific. In this account, God blesses men and women and says to them "Be fruitful and multiply, and fill the earth and subdue it; and have dominion over the fish of the sea, and over the birds of the air, and over every living thing that moves upon the earth."

But there's another account of creation that demands our attention. Genesis 2:4-15 tell a different story. There are not seven days, just one day. The writer of this older account, whom we call the Yahwist author, tells the story of God creating the world and humans on the same day. In this account, God reaches down into the soil of creation like a potter reaching for clay. God takes this soil — this arable, good soil from which all things have grown, and blows life into the human.[2] It is not dirt! I have been instructed by our congregation's scientists that dirt is what you sweep with a broom; soil isn't what is used for creation. Some versions use the word "dust," but the word in Hebrew is *adamah*, which is better translated as fertile soil. God uses *adamah* (arable soil) to create *adam*, the man. The human is formed with close connection to the soil. We have, as theologian Ted Hiebert has said, "the same status" as all other life.[3]

In the movie, *The Lorax*, which is based on the book by Dr. Seuss, a boy falls in love with a girl who only wants one thing: to see a live tree. The world they live in is devoid of nature. Trees have been destroyed, plowed under for progress. Some criticize the movie's political statements, but the larger issue of deep relationship and human responsibility for polluting the earth cannot be ignored.

With all the trees gone, the characters are less human. The Lorax, who is the guardian of the forest, had left a single word of warning, "Unless." *Unless* nature is preserved, we are not in relationship with God. *Unless* we heed the words of scripture to abide in deep relationship with creation, we will be less than who God calls us to be. *Unless* we take a hike and meander through creation, we may not see how damaged it has become.

We are, as the Presbyterian "A Brief Statement of Faith" says, "entrusted" with the care of this planet. We are called to live in connection and relationship to all of creation. We are part of a web, interrelated to our other co-creatures. That is our sacred calling: to remain connected to all creation. Unless we do this, that shalom, peace, harmony that God intended for creation from the very beginning will disappear.

In response, listen again to the Yahwist's story of creation from Genesis 2:5-15. See how it is that the human being, formed from the very stuff of earth, has been entrusted with the care of God's creation:

> *In the day that the Lord God made the earth and the heavens, when no plant of the field was yet in the earth and no herb of the field had yet sprung up — for the Lord God had not caused it to rain upon the earth, and there was no one to till the ground; but a stream would rise from the earth, and water the whole face of the ground — then the Lord God formed man from the dust of the ground, (Hebrew: "ha-adamah") and breathed into his nostrils the breath of life; and the man became a living being (Hebrew: "ha-adam.") And the Lord God planted a garden in Eden, in the east; and there he put the man whom he had formed. Out of the ground the Lord God made to grow every tree that is pleasant to the sight and good for food, the tree of life also in the midst of the garden, and the tree of the knowledge of good and evil.*
>
> *A river flows out of Eden to water the garden, and from there it divides and becomes four branches. The name of the first is Pishon; it is the one that flows around the whole land of Havilah, where there is gold; and the gold of that land is good; bdellium and onyx*

> *stone are there. The name of the second river is Gihon; it is the one that flows around the whole land of Cush. The name of the third river is Tigris, which flows east of Assyria. And the fourth river is the Euphrates.*
>
> *The Lord God took the man and put him in the garden of Eden to till it and keep it.*

From the very beginning, the garden of Eden was meant to be a place of safety, relationship, and harmony.

This year, we planted a backyard garden and tilled the soil, celebrating our relationship to the earth. We amended the soil and created a good garden — it wasn't Eden, but it wasn't bad. We planted a zucchini plant, and the plant grew — throwing vines over the fence, outside the garden. I was convinced we would have hundreds of zucchini — *unless*.

But then we did the impossible: somehow the plant died. We did not get a single zucchini from our garden. We had tomatoes, basil, rosemary, peppers... but no squash. I believe that this was part of a larger plot by members of the family who do not like zucchini. Or perhaps... perhaps we failed to care for the garden. Perhaps we did not live up to our role as gardeners.

Our actions in the world should reflect who God calls us to be. Our lives and our actions should be aligned with the music of God's creation.

That is what God calls us to do: to move forward in joy, to pay attention to the song of creation. Let the beauty of God's creation fill you with joy — and then remember that unless we stay in connection to that creation, we will be less than the people God, in Jesus Christ calls us to be.

---

1. Barbara Brown Taylor, *Leaving Church* (San Francisco: HarperCollins, 2006), p. 109.
2. "This is God's Wondrous World," inclusive language text of "This is My Father's World," words by Malthie Davenport Babcock, 1901, alt.; traditional English melody adapted by Franklin L. Sheppard, 1915 and Stanley Oliver, 1929. Published in Voices United: The Hymn and Worship Book of the United Church of Canada, 1996. [Text and music in the public domain.]

3. Theodore Hiebert, "Eden: Moral Power of a Biblical Landscape," in *Moral Landscape of Creation*, Christian Reflection (Waco, Texas: The Institute for Faith and Learning, Baylor University, 2002), pp. 9-16.

Questions for Reflection
1. As inhabitants of God's good garden, what are some ways we can improve our interdependence with other creatures?
2. Compare two translations of Genesis 2. Read first from the more commonly read NRSV, and then consider the translation used in the sermon from the recently released Common English Bible (CEB). Note the differences and consider what it might mean to understand human beings as being created from arable soil instead of "dust." If we share the same status as all other life forms, what implications does that have for our interaction with the Earth?
3. According to the Presbyterian Church (USA)'s confession, "A Brief Statement of Faith," human desire has not always been in accord with God's plan for creation. The statement asserts: "But we rebel against God; we hide from our Creator. Ignoring God's commandments, we violate the image of God in others and ourselves, accept lies as truth, exploit neighbor and nature, threaten death to the planet entrusted to our care. We deserve God's condemnation. Yet God acts with justice and mercy to redeem creation…" As you walk around observing the beauty of creation, what signs do you see of our negative impact on creation? Where do you notice signs of God's justice and merciful redemption?

Take Action
1. Invite your congregation to "take a hike" and celebrate God's creation. Plan a visit to a nearby park or nature preserve. Do research ahead of time about the types of plants and animals native to the area. Take a moment in silent prayer, giving thanks for the magnificent creation at your doorsteps.
2. Plan in advance to hold a worship outside one Sunday. Use Earth-honoring liturgies and hymns and make a joyful noise to God! Some state conservation agencies provide inexpensive tree seedlings that can be given to children or families for home planting.

3. Do your church grounds provide potential habitat for wildlife? Consider ways that members could become involved in helping create a backyard wildlife sanctuary on your church property.

Chapter Four

Paths of Danger

Psalm 29; Luke 8:22-25

Storm Sunday
On the worship table this morning are indications of storms. A grey-colored cloth covers the rocks and plants of creation like a cloud. The tall vases contain blue-tinted water and clouds of shaving cream that drip droplets of stormy water during worship. Storms are paths of danger for disciples, who must discern God's presence in the chaos of life, and respond faithfully through worship and praise, attuning our lives to the one whose power inspires us to say, "Glory!"

Last spring, a parent of one of our daughter's preschooler students told her that her child was a bit apprehensive about thunderstorms. Unfortunately, that was during the time when the tornado sirens were sounding nightly and most of us were spending our evenings in the basement. The lessons of those evenings were deeply imprinted on this little girl's mind. On the morning after one of those horribly loud, earth-shattering storms, the little girl came to school and ran up to Christine. You could tell she was upset. "Miss Christine! Miss Christine! Wasn't that a horrible tomato storm last night?"

Can you imagine just how dreadful a tomato storm would be?

Storms, with or without tomatoes, are scary and unsettling. We have watched the rage of Sandy bear down on the Atlantic coast. We have witnessed destruction in Texas, Kansas, Oklahoma, and many other states. There's been flooding in Colorado. *USA Today* recently reported that scientists are predicting an increase in "robust" and higher-intensity storms over the next several years.[1]

It's hard to imagine. The evidence is becoming irrefutable that humans have influenced these changing weather patterns. In May, scientists announced that heat-trapped gas in the earth's atmosphere passed levels not seen for millions of years. It's a complex issue, but one that certainly invites reflection on the rhetorical question from Psalm 8: "What are human beings that you are mindful of them, mortals that you care for them?"

More and more evidence is showing that human activity has had an impact on these changing weather patterns.

Between 1980 and 2012, the US alone endured 123 storms that each created at least $1 billion in damage. In 2011 alone, there were twelve such storms — the most ever. The wildness of nature just seems to become ever wilder.

Is there a way to hear God's voice in these paths of danger?

We also know the impact of storms on our lives. In his book, *Suburban Junky*, Jude Hassan talks about the path of danger in his life as he became addicted to heroin in high school. Jude grew up right next door to our church and went to high school with many of our kids. His voice is important for us to hear because he reminds us of what is at stake when storms invade our lives. The choices we make can lead to incredible disasters.

In scripture, storms are both signs of danger and reminders of God's gracious presence and power. Storms affirm the sovereignty of God over nature. In the midst of storms that we discover again our connection to nature, and we hear the wisdom of God's redemption… no wonder all in God's temple shall shout, "Glory!"

At first, Psalm 29 may sound a bit like scriptural weather report. Listen to the verbs: "God's glory *thunders* over mighty waters; Yahweh's voice *breaks* the cedars; the voice of Yahweh *flashes* forth flames of fire." The Psalm continues: God's voice *shakes* the wilderness, shakes Kadesh. When God speaks, the oaks *whirl*; it *strips* bare the forests. Then comes the response? "And in his temple all say, "Glory!" (Psalm 29:5-9).

Years and years ago, my wife and I cuddled on a swing on her parent's front porch, watching a Kentucky thunderstorm move across the area. I don't remember what I was thinking, though I know it didn't have anything to do with climate change. With God's incredible light and sound show playing in the background,

I took her hand and asked her to marry me. Maybe the thunder scared me! My emotional response to the storm wasn't far from the experience of the psalmist. In the midst of God's power, the psalmist is moved to see how God is moving across the landscape of our lives.

What we witnessed that evening could not have been described by even the most eloquent of weather forecasters. Even the articulate Al Roker lacks sufficient words to describe the movement of God in storms. But thankfully we have the words of the psalmist, whose spirit captures the mysteries of God in poetry. As the psalmist describes, God is never far from us in paths of danger.

There's a tendency to blame either God or the TV weather forecasters for the weather. People ask me to pray for a nice day and I tell them, "I'm in sales, not production." Tragically, some try to associate the storms of the world with God's punishment for sin. But what I hear in the words of scripture is a word about the wisdom of God that redeems our lives, a wisdom that stays with us, a presence that remains even as storms invade.

Perhaps this is how we are called to celebrate creation on "storm Sunday." It is a reminder, in the words of Saint Teresa of Avila that "if we learn to love the earth, we will find labyrinths, gardens, fountains, and precious jewels. A whole new world will open itself to us. We will discover what it means to be truly alive."

In the first sermon, I suggested that it was time to dive into the ocean of God's creation; last week I told you take a hike — something I've wanted to say in a sermon for quite some time! Today, with these symbols of storm, wind, and rain vividly portrayed in scripture and art, I tell you: be still.

Be still. As storms rage around and within you, discover the presence of God that calms the sea and restrains the overwhelming chaos. Be still: even as you are battered by winds of struggle and change. Be still: even during seasons of change in your lives, times when the dark storm clouds drench your spirits. Be still, and discover the promise of God that evokes wonder, praise, and trust. Be still, so that in the face of global or personal crisis, you may discern God's wisdom, God's peace, God's glory.

As the disciples pushed out into the lake that night, they could see the storms coming. Despite this, as they shoved off into the lake, Jesus settled in against the bow and took a nap. This was no time for sleeping! The dark clouds were forming, the wind began to blow quickly, and suddenly the waves were pushing against the little boat. The disciples were panicked — how could he be asleep in a time like this?

The disciples were terrified. Yet Jesus was still — enfolded deep in the promise of God's rest. Don't be shocked: He was still, but that did not mean he was out of touch with what was happening. It's the old adage: In times of crisis, don't just do something, stand there. Stand there as the waves are lapping into the boat and believe that God is still at work. Stand there, trusting the one who is leading us through the storm. Indeed, in the words of that great spiritual: The storm is passing over!

We have witnessed the power of catastrophic storms, and it should give us pause. We may rejoice that God is present in the face of a storm and be thankful that God's people are generous in responding to those afflicted by disaster. Yet, we may also wish to be still and consider the impact of our human activity on deadly weather patterns.

It isn't that Jesus had read the weather reports, or that he was more skilled at understanding cloud formations. Rather, Jesus understands the power of God that brings redemption to our lives. It was God's voice that hovered over the unformed chaos of creation; it was God who led the people of Israel through the waters of the sea, and it is God who remains in control at this moment. He is bold in his response, and he called the disciples also to be bold.

Where is your faith?

A year after we watched that storm roll in over the green Kentucky hillside, my wife and I were married. All seemed promising and strong. Our first year of married life was wonderful and filled with joy — until the day when my father was diagnosed with cancer. We knew he'd been sick, but otherwise we had not seen this storm coming. And it was the "perfect storm." Surgery weakened his body, which created more problems. The clouds formed, the winds stirred. We saw him at Christmas, but just a few weeks before our graduation from seminary, the storm of cancer overwhelmed my dad. While our friends were studying for finals, we were preparing to bury my dad on our first anniversary — just months after his 65th birthday.

I felt as though the storms had overwhelmed me. It wasn't fair. It wasn't his time. It wasn't right. The boat of our family life filled with water.

In the midst of all of this, I received a note from Dr. Frieda Gardner, a professor at Princeton and a pioneer in Christian education who would eventually become moderator of the General Assembly of the Presbyterian Church (USA). In a brief note, Dr. Gardner said this: "In time, I pray that you will come to see your father as being closer to you than he was during his life." It was a bold reminder, and an invitation to become calm during the worst storm ever.

---

1. "Study: Climate Change Pumps Up Risk of Severe Storms," *USA Today*. http://www.usatoday.com/story/weather/2013/09/23/climate-change-global-warming-thunderstorms-tornadoes/2854979/

Questions for Reflection
1. Psalm 29 provides a reminder of God's sovereignty in the midst of storms. Yet this may be hard to understand especially as we observe continued destruction in the wake of catastrophic storms. The recent typhoon in the Philippines provides yet another example of calamity striking a vulnerable people. In your experience, how is God present in the midst of chaos? Can we speak authentically of a God who is present, despite destruction and pain?
2. Have you ever watched the wind blow, the rain fall, or lightning strike and said, "Glory"?
3. When we say, "this too shall pass," are we sharing the collective wisdom of those who have experienced life-altering disaster or are we avoiding difficult questions about the presence of God in struggle.

Take Action
1. What is your congregation's disaster plan? Are ushers or staff members prepared to assist worshipers in the event of a tornado?

2. Has anyone in your church considered what might happen if a tornado/fire/flood might incapacitate church members? One resource for consideration is Community Arise, which includes a self-paced online study of developing a congregational action plan. It's available at www.communityarise.com.

3. Consider encouraging members to donate materials for clean-up kits containing supplies used by disaster victims. Visit http://www.cwsglobal.org/get-involved/kits/emergency-clean-up-buckets.html for more information on Church World Service's clean-up bucket ministry.

Chapter Five

Bread from Heaven

Psalm 148; Colossians 1:15-20; John 6:41-51

Cosmos Sunday
Jesus said, "I am the living bread that came down from heaven…" His words are an invitation to come to the Eucharistic table giving thanks for creation, while also recalling that God intends this bread for the entire world. The gift is not just for us.

In the worship space today are reminders of God's cosmos. Stars and planets are suspended over the congregation. As we gather at the Lord's Table, we lift up our heads in praise, delighting in God's creation, thanking God for the gift of life in Jesus Christ.

My mother, who will be 91 in a few weeks, called me the other day. Mom doesn't call us all that much anymore, and so when she does I know that she has something important on her mind. That day she wanted to talk about World Communion Sunday — which we celebrate today.

It's always been one of her favorite Sundays. She was trying to remember when World Communion Sunday began to be celebrated. She holds a vivid memory of her pastor in the 1930s leading their Presbyterian church in communion — reminding them that even in a time of global uncertainty, Christ was calling them to break bread and lift the cup with brothers and sisters around the world. It is on this day that we celebrate our oneness with all who call upon Christ.

When I got off the phone with my mom, I remembered that my theological education didn't begin (or end) at Princeton. It began at home. What we celebrate today began in Pittsburgh in 1933, when the Reverend Hugh Thomson Kerr brought an idea to his congregation. He was looking for some visible expression of invisible unity in Jesus Christ. Today, as we consider ourselves in relationship to all of creation, we join with Dr. Kerr's longing that in Jesus Christ all of creation would stand in thankful praise.

As we celebrate creation, we're led to see possibilities within God's creation we never expected or imagined we would find. We're led to a deeper communion with creation, better equipped to praise God, and better empowered to discern God's ecological wisdom. To me, that is good news.

When we dove deep into the ocean we were able to see the beauty of God's creation in our oceans. We were invited to take a hike and listen for the song of creation in the chirping of birds and the chuffing of animals. In the face of storms, God calls us to be still, and we sense God's protection. Today, we are called to lift up our heads.

Lift up your heads! See the glory of God in the cosmos. Look at the sky, the sun, the moon, the stars of night. This is our call to worship on World Communion Sunday — to join all of God's creation in praise. Hear again Psalm 148:

> *Praise God, sun and moon; praise God all you shining stars! Praise God you highest heavens, and all you waters above the heavens. Let them praise the name of the Lord, for he commanded and they were created! Mountains and all hills, fruit trees and all cedars, wild animals and all cattle, creeping things and flying birds.*

If fruit trees and hills can sing, if storms and sky and seas can praise their Creator, then we ought not to sit still in worship. Worship is a time of giving and of receiving new perspectives. The late Jewish theologian Abraham Heschel once observed that humans are the "cantors of the universe." In other words, you had better accept the director's pleas to sing in the choir because one day you will be singing in heaven! We need all the rehearsals we can get! God yearns to hear our praise. Sing praise to God for we are valued members of God's choir.

But if the air is polluted, how can it sing? If creeks run dry, how can they praise? If the oceans are clogged with debris, how can they rejoice? If humans believe we are the center of the universe, how can we give thanks for God's gift? From the very beginning of this Psalm, it is clear that humans are called to reflect on their deep calling to act as God's stewards of our earthly home. Lift up your heads, and see the gift God has given us.

It was that sort of perspective that changed astronaut, and Presbyterian, Buzz Aldrin's experience of creation into an experience of communion. When *Apollo 11* landed on the moon in 1969, astronauts Neil Armstrong and Buzz Aldrin prepared to touch the moon's surface. Before they left, however, Aldrin, a Presbyterian, silently gave thanks to God, and then did something he had quietly planned with his pastor. Stowed away on the Lunar module were packets of bread and wine, along with a chalice given to Aldrin by his Presbyterian Church in Texas. Aldrin said:

> *I poured the wine into the chalice our church had given me. In the one-sixth gravity of the moon the wine curled slowly and gracefully up the side of the cup. It was interesting to think that the very first liquid ever poured on the moon, and the first food eaten there, were communion elements. And so, just before I partook of the elements, I read the words, which I had chosen to indicate our trust that as man probes into space we are in fact acting in Christ. I sensed especially strongly my unity with our church back home, and with the Church everywhere. I read: "I am the vine, you are the branches. Whoever remains in me, and I in him, will bear much fruit; for you can do nothing without me"* (John 15:5).[1]

The psalm calls us into communion, which also raises some amusing practical issues. How exactly does this all work? Cedar trees aren't able to join praise bands, nor are there sea monsters in the church choir. There are no wild animals who sing tenor, nor creeping things wearing choir robes. So how does this whole ensemble of God strike up the beat? From the start it appears that it is humans who are called to pick up the baton. We are called to see, to sing, and to strike up the hallelujah chorus. "We are," says theologian Bill Brown "the conductor of God's cosmic symphony."[2]

We are the drum majors, the directors, the leaders of God's chorus. Too often, however, we're out of step. We're not marching to the beat of creation, like the crowds who clamored around Jesus. They were confused, out of step. They could not see with the eyes of faith. As he looked at the crowds in the wilderness, Jesus yearned for them to understand what it would be like to lift up their heads, to sing praise to God, to join in conducting God's symphony. He told them that he was the bread they needed to eat in order to hear the beats of God's love — yet they did not understand. He was calling them into deep relationship, into communion with creation and each other. But when they looked around they didn't understand. They failed to understand, so once more he pointed to himself and said "I am the living bread."

If we are to receive that bread, then we ought to discover what it means to be united with all of God's people. To be part of a world communion means that we lift up our heads not in triumph, but in humility. In humility, we look around to make certain all have enough of the living bread. It means, as Sallie McFague argues, recalling we are all relational beings, not "just self-interested individuals." She continues by noting that humans are "primarily communal beings who become unique individuals through help from and response to others."[3] We are beings in community, and we cannot flourish if all other creatures on earth are failing to thrive.

Lift up your heads — and begin to hear the chorus of praise. Join in that magnificent hymn of praise:

> *This is God's wondrous world,*
> *I rest me in the thought of*
> *Rocks and trees and skies and seas,*
> *God's hand the wonders wrought.*

In his book, *Stations of the Heart*, Richard Lischer tells the story of his son's terminal illness. At one point, he and his son get into a discussion about the Eucharist. Adam, his son, has become a Catholic and participates in daily mass. He tells his Lutheran father that in the face of illness, communion has new meaning for him. He says, "You come to the altar and give God everything you have, and God gives you everything he has. You say to God, 'This is my body, and you bring it like a piece of bad meat.' God says, 'No, this is my body.' "[4]

And then God gives you living bread. God's love in Jesus Christ — the bread that is offered for the world — comes to you. That is the bread given to us for our redemption, and for the redemption of the world. It is for all who are hungry, and it is for a creation at risk.

Look at those stars! Get out in the night sky and lift up your heads! Join in offering praise with the vastness of creation. As you do, you will be united to all of creation. Lift up your heads — and receive this bread from heaven.

---

1. http://www.ericmetaxas.com/writing/essays/buzz-aldrin-guideposts-article-full-text/.
2. http://www.workingpreacher.org/craft.aspx?m=4377&post=2641
3. Sallie McFague, *Life Abundant* (Minneapolis: Fortress Press, YEAR), p. 110.
4. Richard Lischer, *Stations of the Heart* (City, State: Publisher, Year), p. 105.

Questions for Reflection
1. Psalm 148 is an invitation for all creation to join in acts of praise — straight down to the sea monsters, wild animals, and all creeping things. Can the howling coyote lift its voice in praise? Is the incessant song of the late summer cicadas a horn of praise to God? What voices do we invite to join us in praising God and which voices do we exclude?
2. Some voices are more pleasing than others. Yet the psalmist's roll call of worshipers is not limited only to the kings, princes, and royalty of the world. "Old and young alike" are called to worship — but often our Sunday morning services exclude children. How do we encourage the participation of all at the table of Christ?
3. The psalm may also be seen as delighting in God's gift of biodiversity. As we think of species that are at risk of extinction, is the praise of God somehow reduced? Does the psalm encourage an equality of existence between human and non-human voices?

4. Reflect on this quote from *Keeping and Healing the Creation* by the Presbyterian Church (USA) Eco-Justice Task Force: "In our time the church must fully incorporate the keeping and healing of the creation — the protection and restoration of the vulnerable and the oppressed, both human and nonhuman, into its life and mission."* What steps could your congregation take to live into this vision?

Take Action
1. Check to see if your community has an astronomy club or contact a local planetarium to find out about amateur astronomy organizations. Invite an astronomer to your church or someplace where a group can gather to watch the night sky. Set up telescopes and learn which constellations are currently visible. This could be a wonderful intergenerational event!
2. Rebecca Barnes-Davies suggests a practice of connecting Eucharist with our daily diet. In her book *50 Ways to Help Save the Earth*, Barnes-Davies suggests providing homemade, local, and/or organic bread and grape juice for communion, and suggests worship leaders consider how our Eucharistic liturgies might offer thanks for the gifts of all creation.

*The Committee on Social Witness Policy of the Presbyterian Church (U.S.A.), *Keeping and Healing Creation* (Louisville: 1989), p. 60.

Chapter Six

Charged with Grandeur

Psalm 8; Genesis 1-2

Copied on the front of the bulletin were verses from Gerard Manley Hopkins' poem, "Charged with Grandeur." A globe was placed on a table near the front, emphasizing human's place in the world. Video footage from NASA accompanied the sermon in order to reinforce how we are called to claim our vocation as stewards of creation. Images of an old car and glimpses of the Earth from space were also used as visuals.

Go outside tonight. Go out and look up into the sky. Go out and see the majesty of God's creation. Find a place that is dark enough so that you can see what the psalmist saw. Look up into the heavens, and get lost in wonder.

Not long ago, scientists at NASA discovered what paparazzi have been hunting: young adolescent stars. But I'll give you a clue: Their names were not Justin Bieber or Selena Gomez. The pictures are out of this world, however.

Here's what they found.

Thanks to the Hubble telescope, elegant galaxies billions and billions of years away from the Earth have popped into view. For the last decade, Hubble has been snapping up photographs of these galaxies like a celebrity-chasing photographer. The views are stunning.

And now they are more colorful than ever. Previously, the deep-space images were only captured in the satellite's near-infrared capability. But recently scientists added ultraviolet light to the images — creating the most detailed and vibrant space photograph ever.[1]

This image is not wide, but it is infinitely deep — it stretches back to just a few hundred million years after the big bang. What you see in this image are stars in their early years of formation. These stars were forming five to ten billion years ago. (*A slide of the image was projected on a screen.*)

Let that stay with you, and hear again Psalm 8:

> *O Lord, our Sovereign, how majestic is your name in all the Earth. You have set your glory above the heavens, out of the mouths of babes and infants you have founded a bulwark because of your foes, to silence the enemy and the avenger. When I look at your heavens, the work of your fingers, the moon and the stars that you have established; what are human beings that you are mindful of them?*

Look at the sky.

It is indeed a reminder of what Gerard Manley Hopkins once wrote: "The world is charged with the grandeur of God."[2]

NASA also recently released a video of another spectacular space event. This video[3] shows the eruption of a massive solar flare. Solar flares — also known as coronal mass ejections — are fairly routine events. What is amazing about this video is that it was the first time a solar satellite had recorded an eruption. The IRIS (Interface Region Imaging Spectograph) satellite captured the event last month. Look at this explosion. (*A video of the explosion was shown.*)

This eruption moved at about 1.5 million miles per hour, so obviously NASA has slowed it down to reveal the details. It was equal to five Earths in width and seven and a half Earths in height.

God's galaxies stir our hearts, prompting us to be filled with wonder. Like the psalmist, we may exclaim, "What are human beings that you are mindful of them?" Or, as a character in John Green's book *The Fault in Our Stars*[4] says, "some infinities are bigger than other infinities."

Both the creation account in Genesis 1 and Psalm 8 stir our hearts because they remind us first of God's great love toward human beings. God takes notice of us. According to Genesis, God delights in creation, calling it good, blessing it in love. The psalm reminds us that God is not unattached or removed from creation. God not only cares for creation, God cares for each part of creation. God cares for me. God cares for you.

We bear the image of God in every breath we take. In Jesus Christ, we behold God's love for us and that is very, very good news.

That is what the psalmist affirms: We are only a little lower than God. One of the joys of ministry is helping people reflect on that idea, but it comes with a hard challenge. Our challenge is to remember that not only is the world charged with the grandeur of God, but also that God gives human beings authority in creation. "You have given them dominion over the works of your hands." And it seems to me that one of our purposes as a church — one of the things that God has called us to do in Jesus Christ — is to help people reclaim that identity.

In the Jewish tradition, part of that work has become called *tikkun olam*, or "healing the world." That is the identity we need to reclaim. We need to reclaim our calling to bring healing to the Earth because we have lost track of what it means to "have dominion." In terms of the environment, we have spoiled God's creation by acts of selfishness and unthoughtful ways of caring. We have declared that "having dominion" means being in charge. It has been translated as being owners, not stewards. But the psalmist understood things differently. Dominion was not domination — dominion was participating as God's agent, to act as God would act.

As the psalmist suggests, when we stare into space, when we see the stars and the infinite gap between humans and our Creator, we realize that our work is to declare, "How majestic is your name in all the Earth!"

God is love. God acts in loving and merciful ways. God looks at creation, at all that exists and proclaims it good. To have dominion means that we remember God's covenant, and that we act in ways that do not exalt ourselves over other aspects of creation. We remember that we are in relationship with all of creation. It is that important.

So look at creation. See it for the incredible mystery that it is. At that moment, in the face of its beauty, ask yourself, "What does it mean for us to bear the image of God in this world?"

It makes a difference how we answer that question. One way to answer it is to say that by bearing the image of God in the world, we exercise complete control over the Earth. Dominion has been given to us, so let's dominate! But if we believe we are in complete control of the Earth, then I believe we are going to be greatly mistaken.

At seventeen, I believed that all my problems had been solved as my parents dropped the keys to a 1977 Plymouth Fury into my hands. Do you know how many people you can fit inside a Plymouth Fury? This car was the size of Lake Michigan. Six large adults could sit comfortably inside of it, which translated into about ten teenagers, depending on how friendly they were. And with the keys in my hands, I knew I was in charge.

Where did I go? I loaded the car with my friends and went to Disneyland! I was in charge!

But then the car fell apart, so I decided that the answer was to go to college so I could get a job so I could fix my problems. But after college and seminary, I got married, and then we had a couple of children, and all we could afford was another old car. Then I decided that my problems would be fixed as soon as the kids got older — but then they got older and pretty soon I was the one handing the keys to a clunky old car into the hands of a teenager, praying it wouldn't fall apart.

The point is, it's a fallacy to think that because we're in charge humans can do anything we want, or that God is not concerned with how we care for creation. Did you hear recently that so much trash has accumulated on Mt. Everest that some climbers have called it the world's highest dump? Or have you heard about the floating islands of plastic that fill our oceans?

And yet God is mindful of us.

Our understanding of being made in the image of God and acting as God's stewards needs to be reconsidered. If we think we are the owners of creation — if we think that being in charge will solve our problems, then why worry about it? We can always fix it later. But sooner or later we discover that the world is not ours to trample, and that only as we stand in relationship with all creation will we fulfill what God yearns for us. We were created in God's image — and called to bear that image in the world.

"The world is charged with the grandeur of God," so let us bear that image in all we do. Amen.

---

1. http://www.engadget.com/2014/06/06/hubble-deep-space2014/ accessed 25 June 2014.
2. Gerard Manley Hopkins, "God's Grandeur."
3. See http://www.nasa.gov/mission_pages/iris/
4. John Green, *The Fault in Our Stars* (New York: Dutton Penguin Publishers, 2012), p. 189.

Questions for Reflection
1. Working in pairs, read Psalm 8 together, alternating verses. What new ideas are prompted by hearing the psalm read this way? The psalm is structured so that it guides the readers from the act of praising God toward the exploration of human vocation, and then back to an acclamation of praise.
2. Psalm 8 has been described as a "psalm for stargazers." It captures the experience of discovering the distance between God's grandeur and the seeming insignificance of a human being. Does worship provide you with a chance to glance at God's grandeur?
3. Humans are given a profound vocation. How does your congregation communicate the good news that people matter?
4. Review Deuteronomy 17:14-20 which outlines the limits of royal power. What do these limits suggest about dominion being a sacred responsibility rather than an invitation to exploit as desired?

Take Action
1. Consider planting a community garden. Involve the congregation in the planning and logistics, and recruit assistance from neighbors. Link the garden to the human vocation of caring for each other by growing produce for a local food pantry.
2. Another possible activity is to build a greenhouse using recycled plastic soda bottles. There are numerous websites that provide instructions and illustrations of this activity. If your church lacks space, contact one of your denomination's camp or retreat centers to see if they would consider allowing you to build a greenhouse.

Chapter Seven

What Sort of Animal Are We, Anyway?

2 Corinthians 5:14-21

A Communion Meditation

Lisa Simpson, Bart's saxophone playing sister, is a big-hearted environmentalist. In a classic episode, Lisa discovers that an oil tanker has crashed, spilling thousands of gallons of oil on a beach. Wildlife has been endangered. The situation is urgent. Lisa pleads with her mother to go and help. They rush to the scene, hoping to save a baby seal or perhaps a cute otter. Yet when they arrive, they discover celebrities got there ahead of them. The stars rushed in, cleaned up the seals, took photos, and left.

All that is left for Lisa and Marge to clean are rocks — thousands and thousands of rocks. Marge sighs deeply. "I've got rocks that need washing at home."[1]

Lisa learns a hard lesson about the human heart. No matter our intentions, no matter how hard we yearn to make a difference in the world, we often crash against the shores of egotism, privilege, or status.

What words best describe human beings?
- cold
- opportunistic
- hopeful
- depressed
- vulnerable
- empathetic
- unfailingly optimistic
- maternal
- nurturing
- murderous

- frivolous
- loving
- faithful

Following the shooting of Michael Brown by police officers in Ferguson, Missouri, we saw not only an explosion of anger, but also grief and pent-up rage. Hearts were wrenched open by raw emotion — disappointment, fear, and grief. There were ample reasons to give up. In the midst of the chaos, clergy and church members walked the streets. Like Lisa, they kept washing the soiled rocks, declaring hope where few saw signs of possibility.

Whatever else we are, humans are complicated animals.

Many of us are deeply empathetic, but also self-centered. We are capable of caring for others, but also willfully narcissistic. In Paul's words, we can be consumed by a desire to serve God, but are also focused on the things of the flesh. Hostile to God, unconcerned with our sisters and brothers, we live for the moment — crashing oil tankers, polluting streams, and stripping forests.

Humans, notes novelist Curtis White, need to discover powers (in his words, "gods") that overcome such barbaric tendencies. "We are," he writes "that strange and wonderful animal that has the metaphysical comfort of knowing that she is part of the tragic chorus of natural beings."[2] The answer to environmental crises, suggests White, comes by way of thoughtfulness — a deep appreciation of the world's beauty, a pondering of its aesthetic virtue.

White is partly right. The answer does indeed come from a thoughtful heart — but more importantly, it comes from a heart that has been transformed by the grace of Jesus Christ. In his letter to the Corinthians, Paul points out that the world and all that is in it groans in anticipation, "longing to be clothed with our heavenly dwellings" (2 Corinthians 5:2). Secure in our hope we remain confident, "for the love of Christ urges us on."

Followers of Christ, says Paul, are not judged by human standards. The bar has been set higher. If anyone is in Christ," Paul writes, "there is a new creation: everything old has passed away; see, everything has become new!" (2 Corinthians 5:17). Everything is new!

Paul's words urge us to live fully in God's grace. We must trust that God's transforming power is already at work in the world, and by our actions in the world show that to be true. He calls the Corinthians to live as if they have had heart transplants.

A heart transformed by grace is indeed a thoughtful heart. It is a heart that has been caressed by Jesus' love so that it can beat in rhythm with the Holy Spirit. It is a heart that circulates the life blood of faith in a faithless world. Such hearts are signs of who we are called to be in Christ. Baptized into hope, we rise from the waters to live as Christ's ambassadors. Satisfied with the meal of the kingdom, we are entrusted with the good news of the gospel — bringing hope in a world choked by pollution, filled with violence, torched by hate.

There are ample reasons to despair over the ways humans have acted in the world. The catalogue of excesses and abuses is thick, and we have memorized large sections of it. Yet, as Paul reminds us, there is in Christ a new creation. Everything is new — including our hearts. We are, as Jennifer Phillips writes, a people "called to live as those who see the cosmos with renewed vision, as showing forth Christ everywhere."[3]

What sort of animals are we, anyway? We are people called by hope, who take the gifts of creation and give thanks to God. We are people called to break the bread and drink the cup, offering our hearts in thanksgiving to God and each other. We are people who do not lose hope, who are "dying… and (yet) alive…" who are seen "as sorrowful, yet always rejoicing; as poor, yet making many rich, as having nothing, and yet possessing everything." We are complicated animals indeed.

Thanks be to God.

---

1. "Bart After Dark," episode 5, season 8, originally airing November 26, 1996.
2. Curtis White, "The Barbaric Heart," *Orion* magazine, May/June 2009.
3. Jennifer M. Phillips, *Preaching Creation Throughout the Church Year* (Cambridge, Massachusetts: Cowley Publications, 2000), p. 41.

Questions for Reflection
1. On a flip chart or marker board, brainstorm ways that God's people are "dying" yet "alive." We are bombarded with messages that attendance is declining among American congregations. That may be so—but how is your church "alive" in spite of declining membership trends?
2. What would adopting an approach of "deep thoughtfulness" look like in your church? Where is there an empathy deficit? In which ways can we expand and encourage our care for creation?

Take Action
1. Depending on your church's polity and practice, appoint a team of members to bring communion to those who cannot attend worship. This could include, but is not limited to, those who are ill and confined to home. It could also include those whose work schedules impact their Sunday morning attendance. As you share the gifts of creation, share stories of hope that reflect God's new creation alive in your ministries.
2. Work with the children and youth of your congregation to create a brief video that explores the theme, "What sort of animal are we?" Create a video collage that can be posted on YouTube or posted on a church Facebook account. Tell stories of hope that allow others to hear how your congregation is involved in sharing God's good news.

Chapter Eight

Uncovering Our Ears

Acts 7:55-60

Sometimes, you hear things you wish you didn't hear.

Not long ago, I was at a business and overheard a woman talking to an employee. The woman was obviously greatly disturbed — but it was also apparent that she was the sort of person who could graciously be described as an "over sharer." Do you know what I mean? Someone had turned on the tap of her soul and everything was spilling out at once. Words came out of her like a leaky garden hose, spilling everywhere. And it was particularly clear that her over-sharing was making the employee uncomfortable.

He kindly moved her toward the exit — but that didn't stop her. The low-down on her personal struggles continued trickling out of her nonstop. The man was getting the nitty-gritty — and somewhat uncomfortable — insider information on her personal struggles. She spared nothing. He tried walking away — but she followed. In desperation, the man looked at her and tried to be upbeat. He placed his arm on her shoulder and said, "Ma'am, all I can I say is just keep looking at Jesus!" That finally caught her, and she paused for a moment. He didn't hesitate, "Like I said, just keep looking at Jesus!"

I'm not sure if it was the answer she was looking for, but it did manage to keep her quiet.

Stephen — full of grace and truth — kept looking at Jesus. His eyes never wavered, though no one wanted to hear what he was saying. Stephen kept telling the story of Jesus, even when the crowd didn't want to hear what he had to say. Sweet, angel-faced Stephen kept sharing a message no one wanted to hear.

The truth is that sometimes the truth is rather hard to accept.

Some years ago, I made a hospital visit on a church member. Dave had been fighting cancer for years. It had been a tough road — the cancer was particularly vicious in the way it grew tumors on muscles and in the lining of his abdomen. But Dave was young and committed to fighting back against cancer. He insisted he would not give up.

When I walked into his room that day, I could tell the tide had turned. To use Malcolm Gladwell's phrase, Dave had reached a tipping point. He was exhausted, weakened by the constant bombardment of chemo. As I sat down, he told me, "The doctor is coming and I want you to stay and hear what she says."

Of course the news wasn't good. The doctor was kind, professional, and direct. She flatly told him there were no other treatment options. The cancer could not be stopped, and Dave was going to die. He shook his head as if to say, "I'm not listening."

While he eventually came to terms with his terminal diagnosis, I suspect many of us can identify with Dave: Sometimes, the truth is too hard to hear.

I wonder if Stephen felt that way while preaching to the council.

Stephen's sermon had an interesting impact on his congregation. First they stuck their fingers in their ears; then they killed him. Clearly, Stephen's sermon didn't turn out the way the pulpit committee had planned. Stephen might wish to brush up on his Dale Carnegie lessons.

Or perhaps he just needed to keep telling the hard-to-hear truth.

Full of grace and power, not only did Stephen perform great wonders and signs (Acts 6:8), he did the unthinkable. He told the truth.

That was true in Stephen's day and is still true today. Scientists from around the world are working hard to study the Earth's climate changes. Earlier last year, a broad team of researchers released the third National Climate Assessment. More than 300 experts, including representatives from industry, government, and education, were involved in this assessment.

Their conclusion?

Climate change, or global warming, isn't something that might happen someday. It's already underway. And the vast majority of scientists believe humans have had a negative impact on how climate is changing.

Many Americans, however, don't agree. A recent Gallup poll shows only about 34% of Americans worry about climate change. The Pew Research Center has discovered that Americans are outliers on this issue when compared to other nations such as Canada, France, Japan, or Germany. It's clear that not everyone believes the climate is changing — and perhaps that includes some of you. Some see it as a political football or see it as way of generating votes.

I'm not here to argue the politics of global warming. But as one of our astute high school students told me the other day, "Even if it isn't happening the way scientists say, would taking steps to preserve the Earth be such a bad idea?"

Perhaps it's time to uncover our ears and listen for the truth.

Take a moment and listen to the report's findings. The massive report documents the ways climate change is happening today: from droughts to torrential rains, to heat waves and wild brush fires, to melting glaciers and extreme weather events, climate change is part of daily life.

Every part of the United States is impacted by the changing climate. Northern areas are feeling the change at a swifter pace than some other areas, but few places in the United States will go unscathed.

"Americans are noticing changes all around them," the government's National Climate Assessment report notes. "Summers are longer and hotter, and extended periods of unusual heat last longer than any living American has ever experienced.[1] Winters are generally shorted and warmed. Rain comes in heavier downpours." Rising seas will put major seaports at risk.

Here's an illustration: Not long ago, scientists announced that portions of the West Antarctic Ice Sheet have begun to collapse. The researchers called it an "unstoppable" process that over the course of centuries could raise sea levels by fifteen feet. The region seems to be warming more quickly than anticipated.[2]

No part of the United States is immune to these challenges. Scientists nearly universally attribute these changes to increasing levels of human-produced carbon dioxide and fossil fuel emissions. Great changes are underway and it is time to pay attention.

By and large, however, Americans have closed their ears to climate change.

When compared to other nations, Americans tend to see climate change as less of a threat. The Pew poll noted that most Americans view Islamic extremism, Iran's nuclear program, or North Korea as a greater threat than the environment. While all countries will be affected by a changing climate, poorer nations will face greater risks. Concern over climate change in middle or poorer nations is higher than it is in the United States, with only the Middle East not having a majority seeing the issue as a critical threat.

Like the crowd that faced Stephen, climate change skeptics are grinding their teeth. You may not agree with me, and that is okay — just don't start hurling stones. There are valid arguments on both sides of the equation. Let's listen to the scientists, however. Let's listen to our youth — they are deeply interested in the environment. Above all, let us remember that God calls us to be wise stewards of creation.

Perhaps this is an invitation to listen carefully to what science is trying to tell us. Perhaps it is time to uncover our ears.

This week's lectionary passage from Acts 7 plops us down in the middle of the action shortly before Stephen is stoned. It's a gruesome scene, but also a potent reminder of the church's calling to bear witness to uncomfortable truths. The mob has turned on the innocent, angel-faced Stephen.

Stephen describes the mighty acts of God in Israel's history. His sermon recounts the ways God's people had consistently rejected God — rejecting Moses, worshiping idols, reveling in the works of their hands, and forever opposing the Holy Spirit. Stephen gives voice to Luke's unique historical perspective, mushing together a pastiche of times, places, and narratives in order to assert a particular Christological stance. God's people resisted, yet God persisted.[3]

Stephen's sermon races toward its finish line. Along the way, he seals his fate by rattling off this bit of winsome homiletical phraseology: "You stiff-necked people, uncircumcised in heart and ears, you are forever opposing the Holy Spirit, just as your ancestors used to do."

Note to preachers: cut out the "stiff-necked people" line if you're arguing for a raise.

The crowd seizes with anger and grinds their teeth as Stephen concludes, "You are the ones that received the law as ordained by angels, and yet you have not kept it."

It wasn't just an inconvenient truth — it was the plain truth, and yet the crowd was unable to accept it. Even at that moment, Stephen remains full of power and grace. In the face of death, at the feet of his oppressors, Stephen cries out, "Lord do not hold this sin against them."

They must have heard that — because it is mighty hard to cover your ears if you've picked up a rock.

In his commentary on Acts, William H. Willimon notes that the persecution of Stephen was not some isolated act of violence. It represented the shift in the church as its message challenged the status quo. Jesus' followers became the seeds of faith scattered into far-flung regions, but even there God's message is able to bear fruit. Willimon tells of three bronze plaques placed near the MacKay Center at Princeton Theological Seminary. One sees three bronze plaques inscribed with the name of Princeton graduates, who like Stephen, paid for their vision in blood:

Walter Macon Lawrie — Thrown overboard by pirates in the China Sea, 1847.
John Rogers Peal — Killed with his wife by a mob at Lien Chou, China, 1905.
James Joseph Reed — Fatally beaten at Selma, Alabama, March 11, 1965.[4]

Each one, like Stephen, answered a version of the same question, "Are these things so?" Their names, says Willimon, "remind us of some later-day witnesses who went before us, some of whom paid dearly for their witness to the truth."

It could be easy for us to ignore this gruesome story. Yet these verses are a reminder of the church's calling to witness to truth. The preacher is summoned to listen carefully to Stephen's witness, and to imagine how God's people have stopped listening today.

Take note. Who are we in this drama? Are we Stephen, persecuted for giving witness to what we have seen and know to be true? Are we the ones picking up stones? Are we in the crowd, with our fingers covering our ears, grinding our teeth at the sound of Stephen's voice? Or are we Saul, who at this moment seems to be nothing more than a glorified coat-check guy, standing on the sidelines, consenting to the messenger's death?

As we identify ourselves, we may be able to then listen for the promise of redemption. Rather than drowning in the so-called "data of despair" about the environment, perhaps now is the time to uncover our ears, and begin to make even simple changes in the way we care for creation.

Stephen's witness becomes our witness as we encourage our congregations to uncover their ears and listen for the challenge of truth. As a Presbyterian church (USA) policy statement on climate change observes, "The challenge we face is daunting. The temptation to despair is real. Only God can give us the power to change… we can repent of our own sinful misuse and abuse of the Earth as we confess our sins. As recipients of God's endless mercy, this redemptive energy frees and empowers us to be good stewards of God's creation."[5]

It is not easy to proclaim truth. But even stiff-necked people can change. Eventually even Saul will travel the Damascus road. The stones get heavy, and we set them down. Perhaps even those who have yet to hear will begin listening. We can only pray.

---

1. Melillo, Jerry M., Terese (T.C.) Richmond, and Gary W. Yohe, eds., 2014: Climate Change Impacts in the United States: The Third National Climate Assessment. U.S. Global Change Research Program, 841 pp. doi:10.7930/J0Z31WJ2. (See http://nca2014.globalchange.gov/downloads)

2. See http://www.nbcnews.com/science/environment/west-antarctic-ice-sheets-collapse-triggers-sea-level-warning-n103221

3. Beverly Roberts Gaventa, *Acts, Abingdon New Testament Commentary* (Nashville, Tennessee: Abingdon Press, 2003), p. 133.
4. Willimon, *Acts* (Louisville: Westminster/John Knox Press, 1988), p. 65.
5. "The Power to Change: US Energy Policy and Global Warming," Louisville, Kentucky, The Advisory Committee on Social Witness Policy, Presbyterian Church, USA, 2008, p. 23.

Questions for Reflection
1. Any discussion of global warming can easily become "heated." Be sure to follow best practices for holding conversations on controversial topics. Encourage a variety of views to be expressed, but make sure the space is open and accessible to all viewpoints. Ask, "What do you know about climate change?" Why do we resist hearing hard truths?
2. Create a Venn diagram that lists various points of view on climate change. Ask the question, "Has human activity caused climate change?" Show both sides of the debate and look for possible areas of common ground or agreement. (Visit http://www.pbs.org/now/classroom/globalwarming.html for information and ideas about discussions on global warming.) What are the theological reasons for being concerned about global climate change?
3. View the short video, "Bamboo Bikes Initiative: Ghana" from www.ghanabamboobikes.org to see how women from Ghana have built sturdy bicycles from bamboo — creating employment opportunities while also reducing the carbon needed for traditional bicycle production. What does this initiative suggest about human creativity and ingenuity in addressing multiple problems, including climate change?

Take Action
Challenge members of the church or group to measure their carbon footprint by using one of several calculators available on the internet. A footprint is one way of estimating our consumption of resources. Some websites also offer interactive maps that show the varying carbon footprints of different nations and continents.

Chapter Nine

A Festival of Hymns Celebrating Creation

A hymn festival provides another way of introducing Earth care themes to a congregation. This service offers worship planners a choice in balancing new or contemporary songs with traditional hymns. Sources for the hymns are listed below.

"You cannot in one glance survey this most vast and beautiful system of the universe, in its wide expanse, without being completely overwhelmed by the boundless force of its brightness."
— John Calvin, *Institutes of the Christian Religion*

Call to Worship — based on Psalm 96

One: Let the heavens be glad, and let the earth rejoice!
All: Let the sea roar, and all that fills it;
One: Let the field exult, and everything in it.
All: Then shall all the trees of the forest sing for joy before the Lord!
Together: For God will come to judge the world with righteousness, and the peoples with God's truth!

OR

One: Delight in God's goodness, and celebrate God's creation with joy!
All: Sing praises to God, who makes the seas roar, and the sun to rise.
One: Offer to God thanks for every good gift,
All: Let God's glories shine on us in our worship and praise.

Hymn of Praise: (choose from these options)
"Earth And All Stars"
"All Creatures Of Our God And King"
"For The Beauty Of The Earth"
"Morning Has Broken"

Prayer of Confession
How beautiful, O Lord, is your creation! You fill the Earth with good things and have called us to be wise stewards of what you have given. Yet we confess we have abused your creation. We have polluted lakes and streams, and have spoiled the air. We have consumed more than our fair share of our planet's resources and have not acted responsibly in our stewardship. Forgive our foolishness, O God, and broaden our awareness so that we might live more faithfully before you. Hear our prayer in Jesus' name, Amen.

Words of Assurance
Know that the Lord is God; it is God who made us, and we are the sheep of God's pasture. "We know," says Paul, "that the whole creation has been groaning in labor pains until now," and that "in hope we were saved." Brothers and sisters, rejoice and be glad: in Jesus Christ we are forgiven.

Response
"The Trees Of The Field" (Words by Steffi Geiser Ruben; music by Stuart Dauermann)
"Santo, Santo, Santo" (Holy, Holy, Holy) (Traditional Argentine text and music)
"Halle, Halle, Hallelujah" (Text: Marty Haugen; Music Caribbean melody).

Prayer for Illumination
One: Lord our God,
You sent your Spirit to brood over the waters of creation, and breathed into every living being the breath of life. So now fill us with anticipation, as the scriptures are read and your word is proclaimed, we may once more delight in your good creation. Amen.

First Scripture Reading: Genesis 2:4b-9, 15

Hymn
"God Of The Sparrow, God Of The Whale"
"Touch The Earth Lightly" (text by Shirley Erena Murray; music by Colin Gibson)
"I Am Your Mother" (text by Shirley Erena Murray; music by Per Harling)
"How Great Thou Art"
"The River Is Here" (contemporary) (words and music by Andy Park)

Second Scripture Reading: Isaiah 55:6-12

Anthem or Hymn
"Called By Earth And Sky" (Words and music by Pat Mayberry)
"Let All Things Now Living"
"Christ Be Our Light"

Gospel Scripture Reading: Matthew 6:25-34

Hymn
"Blest Are They"
"Let The Whole Creation Cry"
"Joyful, Joyful, We Adore Thee"
"All Over The World" (contemporary; Matt Redman)

Offertory
"We Are An Offering" (Words and music by Dwight Liles)
"Give Thanks" (words and music by Henry Smith)
"Hallelujah! We Sing Your Praises!" (Haleluya! Pelo tsa rona!) (South African)

Prayer of Thanksgiving and Intercession
Gracious God, you have created the world and called it good — every fish that swims in the streams, every antelope that runs in the wild, every child who delights in blowing seeds of a dandelion. It is all so very good, O Lord, and we give you thanks for your gifts.

With gratitude, we raise our spirits to you:
Hear our prayer, O Lord.
We thank you for your care of creation, for the resilience of our earthly home; we are amazed by the diversity of people and animals, rocks, and trees. All of it displays your grandeur and wisdom, and we join our voices to the chorus of heaven in giving you thanks and praise:
Hear our prayer, O Lord.
We offer to you our prayers for creation. All creation groans inwardly as landfills leak toxins, as hillsides erode, and rivers become clogged with debris. We pray for an end to wasteful consumption, and ask your help in becoming better stewards of your treasures. Give to humans a desire for delight in your good works, and a reverence for your gifts, even as we open our hearts to you now:
Hear our prayer, O Lord.
We pray for the animals that share our earthly home. You created each species in wonder and joy, and your thumbprint is evident in each one's life. Teach us to deal generously with the animals in our care; help us to care for our pets; bless service animals with added measures of your grace, and teach us responsibility in agriculture so that all your creation may serve and worship you:
Hear our prayer, O Lord.
Let your glory saturate our being and may your light be reflected in all creation. Let wisdom echo across valleys, and allow the trees of the field to shout your praise. Allow the seed of your good works to grow within us, and nurture in us new reverence for creation, so that all the world may know and rejoice in your holy name. Amen.

Hymn
"We Will Go Out With Joy" (Words and music by Andrew Donaldson and Hilary Seraph Donaldson)
"All Things Bright And Beautiful"
"Let Us With A Gladsome Mind"
"Go My Children, With My Blessing"

Benediction — Psalm 125
One: "Those who trust in the Lord are like Mount Zion, which cannot be moved, but abides forever." Now go forth into God's creation, shouting our praises and delighting in all of God's good works.
All: Amen. Let us go forth in joy!

Sources
Glory to God — The Presbyterian Hymnal (2013)
The Presbyterian Hymnal (1990)
The Faith We Sing (2000)
More Voices (supplement to Voices United: The Hymn and Worship book of the United Church of Canada, 2007)
"The River Is Here" by Andy Park and "All Over The World" by Matt Redman are available from CCLI

Major Sources

Barnes-Davies, Rebecca J. *50 Ways to Help Save the Earth: How You and Your Church Can Make a Difference* (Louisville, Kentucky: Westminster/John Knox Press, 2009).

The Green Bible: New Revised Standard Version (San Francisco, California: HarperOne, 2008).

Hiebert, Theodore. "Creation." *The New Interpreter's Dictionary of the Bible*, Volume 1 (Nashville, Tennessee: Abingdon Press, 2006).

Hiebert, Theodore. "Reclaiming the World: Biblical Resources for the Ecological Crisis." *Interpretation*, Vol. 65, pp. 341-352.

Hiebert, Theodore. *The Yahwist's Landscape* (New York: Oxford University Press, 1996).

Holbert, John C. *Preaching Creation: The Environment and the Pulpit* (Eugene, Oregon: Cascade Books, 2011).

Lane, Belden C. *Ravished by Beauty: The Surprising Legacy of Reformed Spirituality* (New York: Oxford University Press, 2011).

McFague, Sallie. *Super, Natural Christians* (Minneapolis: Fortress Press, 2000).

McFague, Sallie. *Life Abundant* (Minneapolis: Fortress Press, 2000).

Melillo, Jerry M., Terese (T.C.) Richmond, and Gary W. Yohe, eds. *Climate Change Impacts in the United States: The Third National Climate Assessment* (Washington DC: U.S. Government Printing Office, 2014).

Presbyterian Church (U.S.A.), Committee on Social Witness Policy, *Keeping and Healing The Creation* (Louisville, Kentucky: The Presbyterian Church [U.S.A.], 1989).

www.ingramcontent.com/pod-product-compliance
Lightning Source LLC
Chambersburg PA
CBHW071756040426
42446CB00012B/2576